Delicious Ways to Make Carrot Cakes
How To Celebrate Your Holiday

Copyright © 2020

All rights reserved.

DEDICATION

Contents

Triple Decker Carrot Cake

This looks like a traditional carrot cake with walnuts, cinnamon, and of course cream cheese frosting ... but it's more than that. This triple decker carrot cake is super-moist and loaded with carrots, plus the addition of tart Granny Smith apples for more moisture and flavor. The spices in combination with the perfect amount of toasted walnuts is going to send you and your guests to carrot cake paradise.

Ingredients

For the Cake:

1 cup vegetable oil

1 cup, plus 2 tablespoons all-purpose flour

1/2 cup cake flour

1 teaspoon baking powder

1

1 teaspoon baking soda

1/4 teaspoon salt

1 3/4 teaspoons ground cinnamon

1/2 cup brown sugar

1/2 cup granulated sugar

3 tablespoons ground flax seeds

6 tablespoons hot water

1 1/2 teaspoons vanilla extract

4 medium-sized carrots, approximately 2 cups

1 medium Granny Smith apple, peeled

1/4 teaspoon orange zest

3/4 cup toasted walnuts, plus more for garnish

For the Cream Cheese Frosting:

2 cups vegan cream cheese

1/2 cup vegan butter

2 cups confectioner's sugar

1 teaspoon vanilla extract

1 cup vegan buttercream (optional)

For the Buttercream:

1 cup vegan butter

1 cup hi-ratio vegetable shortening

6 cups confectioner's sugar

4 tablespoons non-dairy milk

1 teaspoon vanilla extract

Preparation

To Make the Cake:

Preheat oven to 350°F.

Combine the flax with the hot water and let stand to thicken.

In a large bowl combine the sugars with the oil, vanilla extract and the flax mixture, whisk smooth

Add the orange zest.

Then, sift together all of the dry ingredients directly into the bowl and whisk smooth.

Add the grated carrots and apple and the nuts then mix smooth.

Pour batter into greased 7-inch cake pans and bake for approximately 25-40 minutes depending on the size of your pans. Bake until they are done.

Cool cakes while you prepare the cream cheese frosting.

To Make the Cream Cheese Frosting:

Smooth cream cheese and butter with a paddle attachment.

Add sifted confectioners sugar and blend on low just to combine.

Add extract then add optional buttercream icing.

Mix until smooth.

To Make the Buttercream:

Cream the butter and shortening together with a paddle attachment until light and fluffy, about 5 minutes.

Add the alternative milk of your choice and continue whipping for about 1 more minute.

Add the sifted confectioner's sugar and blend on low until smooth.

Add the vanilla extract.

Blend until smooth.

Notes

Frosting makes 3 cups. You can freeze un-iced carrot cake layers wrapped well for up to one month. Frosted cake must be kept refrigerated but may stay at room temperature for up to 3 hours max.

Raw Carrot Cake With Cashew Lemon Frosting

Three words: vegan carrot cake. Is your mouth watering yet? This seems to be one of those recipes that everybody can enjoy, no matter what their diet preferences are. The cashew lemon frosting adds the perfect amount of tang goodness to the sweetness of the vegan carrot cake base. Top with nuts or seeds for a nice crunch! It is super easy to make; you will just need a food processor and a pan! Serve this cute little treat at a party to impress your guests. This vegan carrot cake is spectacular!

Ingredients

For the Cashew Lemon Frosting

1 1/2 cups cashews

Juice from 1 lemon

2 tablespoons liquid coconut oil

2 tablespoons coconut nectar

1 teaspoon vanilla powder

Water, as needed

For the Carrot Cake

3 large carrots, peeled and chopped into small chunks

1 1/2 cups oats

2 cups dates

1/2 cup dried coconut

1 teaspoon cinnamon

1/2 teaspoon nutmeg

Preparation

To make the frosting: blend all ingredients in your high speed blender until smooth, adding water as needed. Put in the refrigerator.

To make the cake: process the oats into flour in your food processor then throw the rest of the ingredients in the food processor and process until it all begins to stick together.

Assembly: press half the cake mixture into a small spring form pan (mine is about 4 inches). Gently take this out and put on a plate, then put in the freezer until it's solid. Do the same to the remaining half of the cake mixture. Spread about 1/3 of the frosting onto the top of one of the cake layers. Put it in the freezer until the layer of frosting is hard. Place on the other cake layer and frost the entire thing, I let it set in the refrigerator overnight.

Double Decker Carrot Cake

No-bake vegan carrot cake recipe with a silky cashew cream cheese frosting? Yes please! If you like carrot cake, you will love this recipe. Carrots, dates, pineapple, cinnamon, and coconut flakes form the base. Then, it is topped with a sweet creamy cashew frosting. This vegan carrot cake is delicious and healthy! Eat it for any meal of the day!

Ingredients

Cream Cheese-y Frosting:

2 cups soaked cashews

1/4 cup coconut oil

1/2 cup maple syrup

1/2 cup whole coconut milk (from the can)

1/4 cup fermented coconut water or lemon juice

1 tablespoon vanilla extract

1 tablespoon pineapple juice

1 tablespoon lemon juice

Carrot Cake:

4 cups carrot pulp or grated carrot shreds

2 cups pitted dates

1 cup frozen, fresh or canned pineapple (canned will be slightly sweeter but you sacrifice the raw)

1 teaspoon cinnamon

1/2 cup unsweetened coconut flakes

Preparation

Soak cashews for about four hours, then rinse.

Combine all the carrot cake ingredients in a high-speed blender and blend until completely smooth. Scrape down the sides for even blending every minute or so.

Press into a pan (I used an 8-inch springform).

Blend all of the cheesecake ingredients in a high-speed blender on high until completely smooth. This will take a couple minutes blending on high to make completely smooth.

Pour frosting on top of carrot cake.

Refrigerate for more of a frosting consistency or freeze for a more cheesecake consistency for at least 4-6 hours.

Carrot Cake Muffins

With this vegan, no refined sugar and gluten-free muffin version of a classic carrot cake, you won't be able to get enough! It's moist and light and filling at the same time, and with all the spices this recipe is perfect for fall.

Ingredients

1 cup oat flour (you can make your own by blending oats in a high speed blender)

1 cup buckwheat flour

1 1/2 teaspoons cinnamon

1/4 teaspoon nutmeg

1/2 teaspoon ground ginger

1/4 teaspoon vanilla powder (or extract)

1/2 teaspoon baking soda

2 carrots (finelly shredded)

1/2 cup dates (pitted)

1/4 cup maple syrup

2 tablespoons melted coconut oil

1/2 cup coconutmilk

1/4 cup plant milk of choice

1/4 cup finely chopped walnuts or pecans

1/2 cup raisins (optional)

Preparation

Preheat the oven at 350°F.

Combine all ingredients except the nuts and raisnins in a food processor and blend until well combined, but with chunks of carrots.

Fold in the raisins and nuts.

Line a muffin tin with parchment paper or muffin liners and scoop batter into each holder.

Bake the muffins for 25 minutes or until golden brown.

Let them cool.

Dig in!

Pecan Carrot Cake

You can never go wrong with the classics, like this yummy carrot cake! This decadent cake packs carrots, raisins, pecans, and that classic cinnamon flavor with rich cream cheese frosting. Perfect for any occasion or just because.

Ingredients

For the Cake:

2 cups all-purpose flour

3 cups coarsely grated carrot

1/2-3/4 cup golden raisins

3/4 cup brown sugar or coconut sugar

1/2 cup white sugar

1 1/2 teaspoons baking soda

1 teaspoon baking powder

1 flax egg (1 tablespoon ground flax seeds, plus 3 tablespoons water)

3/4 cup avocado oil or vegetable oil

1 teaspoon vanilla extract

4 teaspoons cinnamon

1/2 teaspoon ground cloves

1/2 teaspoon ground nutmeg

1/2 teaspoon ground ginger

A pinch of salt

For the Cream Cheese Frosting:

3 tablespoons vegan cream cheese, room temperature

2 sticks of vegan butter, room temperature

3 teaspoons vanilla extract

2 cups powdered sugar

1/2 cup chopped pecans or walnuts (optional)

Preparation

To Make the Cake:

Preheat oven to 350°F. Grease and flour two 9-inch cake pans. In a medium mixing bowl, whisk together the flour, sugar, cinnamon, ginger, nutmeg, cloves, salt, baking soda, baking powder, and set aside. In a stand mixer fitted with paddle or whisk attachment, beat both sugars with flax eggs on medium-high until combined, about 45 seconds.

Reduce to medium speed and add oil gradually along with the vanilla. Pour the wet ingredients into the dry ingredients and stir them together using a spatula until combined. Stir in the carrots and raisins. Pour into the two 9-inch cake pans and bake for 20-25 minutes. Remove from oven and let cool completely before frosting

To Make the Cream Cheese Frosting:

Beat the cream cheese, butter, and vanilla extract together until they are fully incorporated. Add the powdered sugar gradually and mix until it is smooth and creamy. When frosting the cake, sprinkle the chopped nuts onto the frosting between the layers

Iced Carrot Cake

This carrot cake is a harmonious combination of natural flavors and textures for a delectable spring dessert. So in honor of Easter and the emergence of spring, give this carrot cake recipe a try and enjoy its sweet and delicious taste.

Ingredients

For the Dry Ingredients:

4 medium carrots, peeled and shredded (a food processor makes this step much easier)

3 cups gluten free flour

2 teaspoons baking soda

17

2 teaspoons unrefined salt

1 tablespoon ground cinnamon

Optional 1/4 cup raisins

For the Wet Ingredients:

2 cups unrefined sugar

1 tablespoon molasses

1 tablespoon maple syrup

1 teaspoon vanilla extract

6 tablespoons ground flaxseed mixed with 1 cup water (let sit for ten minutes until thickened)

For the Icing:

1 cup room temp coconut oil or earth balance buttery spread

6 cups powder/castor sugar

1 tablespoon vanilla

1/4 teaspoon unrefined salt

Preparation

First, preheat the oven to 350°F and start by washing then peeling the carrots.

Next finely shred them with a grater or in a food processor for a much easier process.

Add dry ingredients to a medium sized bowl and whisk. Add in the shredded carrots and mix.

Next, combine the ground flaxseed with a cup of water and whisk, set aside for ten minutes. Meanwhile, combine wet ingredients in a separate bowl and taste just in case.

Add the thickened flax-water mix to the wet ingredients, mix, then add wet to dry. Mix until cake batter forms and transfer to two standard sized greased circle pans.

Bake for around 20 minutes or more depending on climate. Just keep checking until a fork inserted comes out clean.

Take out and let cool.

Prepare frosting and once cake has cooled, flip one cake onto a plate and frost.

Next, top with other cake layer and frost that one. Slice, garnish, and serve. Enjoy the sweetness!

Raw Coconut Flour Carrot Cake

Carrot cake is a staple on our dessert menu but when you throw a cream coconut frosting into the mix, you get a truly special cake. This triple-decker treat is moist, delicious, and looks impressive as well.

Ingredients

For the Batter:

2 large carrots, peeled

1/2 cup coconut flour

1/2 cup hemp seeds, peeled

10-12 dates, soaked and pitted

2 tablespoons coconut oil

A pinch of salt

For the Frosting:

2 13.5-ounce cans coconut milk, kept in the refrigerator overnight

Sweetener of your choice, to taste

Preparation

Shred the carrots with a food processor.

Dice the dates with the knife and shred them in the food processor.

Add the other ingredients and process them into an even slightly piecewise "dough".

Divide the batter into three 6-inch, circular cake pans lined with baking paper.

Open the coconut milk and add the solid portion to a bowl. Mix it with the hand mixer at the highest level until a "cream" forms.

Sweeten the frosting to taste and let it chill for 30 minutes.

Finally, cover the whole cake with the frosting and let it cool for 2 hours.

Carrot Cake

This is a wonderful recipe for Easter, children's birthdays, and spring picnics. The frosting can be colored using fruits and vegetables. It turns into a lovely pastel frosting with the carrot juice. You can make it as a cake or as cupcakes (a favorite of children). Find this recipe and more in Raw and Radiant: 130 Quick Recipes and Holistic Tips for a Healthy Life, by Summer Sanders, available from Skyhorse Publishing!

Ingredients

For the Cake:

1 cup grated carrot

1/2 cup grated green apple

1 cup raw organic walnuts, chopped

5 dates, pitted and chopped

1/2 cup coconut flakes

2 tablespoons coconut oil

1/4 cup currants or dried cherries

1/4 teaspoon mesquite powder

1 teaspoon vanilla extract

2 teaspoons ground cinnamon

1 teaspoon grated fresh ginger

1/8 teaspoon grated fresh nutmeg

1 tablespoon lemon juice

1/2 tablespoon lemon or orange zest

1/4 teaspoon sea salt

For the Frosting:

1 cup young coconut meat

1/2 cup coconut butter

1/2 medium banana

1/2 teaspoon vanilla extract

Pinch sea salt

Preparation

For the Cake:

Combine the grated carrot and apple in the food processor and pulse until well combined.

Add the walnuts, dates, coconut flakes, coconut oil, currants, mesquite, vanilla extract, cinnamon, ginger, nutmeg, lemon juice, zest, and sea salt.

Pulse until a cake batter consistency forms. If the batter is too thin, add a little apple juice or water.

Transfer the mixture to desired cake, springform, or cupcake pan.

For the Frosting:

In a blender, combine the coconut meat, coconut butter, banana, vanilla, and salt and blend on high until the mixture is smooth and well combined.

Pour or pipe the frosting onto the cake, spread over the cake, then refrigerate the cake to allow the frosting to firm up and chill.

If you're making cupcakes, use a pastry bag or sandwich bag with a cut tip to decorate.

Walnut Carrot Cake With Cream Cheese Frosting

This Gluten-Free Carrot Cake with Walnuts and Cream Cheese Frosting would make a wonderful dessert for Easter. Or for after Passover. Or for a wedding. Or for any day. Enjoy!

Ingredients

2 ¼ cups gluten-free all-purpose flour mix

1 teaspoon baking powder

1 ¼ teaspoon baking soda

½ teaspoon Kosher salt

2 teaspoon ground cinnamon

½ teaspoon ground nutmeg

½ teaspoon ground ginger

¼ cup ground flaxseed

¾ cup warm water

¾ cup organic sugar

½ cup brown sugar

1 cup canola oil

2 tsp. vanilla extract, divided

Zest of one orange

1/4 cup of fresh orange juice

3 cups carrots, grated

1 ½ cups walnuts, chopped, divided (optional)

12-ounce vegan cream cheese, softened

½ cup vegan butter, softened

3 tablespoons maple syrup, or more to taste

1 ½ – 2 cups powdered sugar, or more to taste

Preparation

Preheat oven to 350 degrees. Grease 2-9 inch cake pans with butter, oil or cooking spray. Line them with parchment paper and then grease the parchment paper. The parchment paper will help you lift the cakes out of the pans. Set aside until ready to use.

In a small bowl, sift together the flour, baking powder, baking soda and salt. Add the cinnamon, nutmeg and ginger and whisk it well so all the dry ingredients are well-combined.

In a large mixing bowl, combine the flaxseed and warm water. Let it sit for 5 minutes until it thickens a bit. To this bowl, add the sugar and brown sugar. Using an electric hand mixer (or your own well-toned muscled arms), start on a low speed and mix the sugar with the flaxseed/water. Add the oil and 1 tsp. of vanilla and mix, starting on low speed and moving up to medium. Next add the orange zest and juice and mix again.

Now slowly add the dry ingredients to the large mixing bowl. I do it in thirds. Add 1/3 of the dry ingredients and beat with the mixer, starting on low speed and building up to high. When the batter is fully mixed, repeat with the second 1/3 and the last 1/3 of the dry ingredients.

Fold in the carrots and ½ cup of the chopped walnuts (if using). You could also add raisins here. I like it best plain or with some walnuts.

Divide the batter between the 2 cake pans and using a spoon, smooth out the top surface. Bake for 35-45 minutes, depending on your oven. Check the cakes at 30 or 35 minutes and see if a toothpick inserted into the middle of the cakes comes out clean. If the toothpick is still wet, bake for another 5 minutes at a time until the cakes are done. It took me 45 minutes total but everyone's oven is different. Gluten-free cakes take longer to bake than gluten cakes (we made a gluten version and it took 30 minutes).

While the cakes are baking, make the frosting. In a large bowl, combine the cream cheese and softened butter and beat with an electric hand mixer. Don't beat it too long because vegan cream cheese tends to get watery. Add the maple syrup and the remaining tsp. of vanilla extract. Add the powdered sugar a little at a time, beating it with the mixer on low and then high speed.

When the sugar has been fully incorporated, taste the frosting. This is important. You're looking for 2 things here: you want the frosting to be as thick as you can get it while also keeping track of how sweet it's getting. I don't like my frosting too sweet so what I used was enough to give me a frosting that was sweet enough and thick enough. For me. You may want it thicker and/or sweeter. Some recipes use up to 6 cups of powdered sugar. Yuck!

When you have the frosting to your liking, cover it with plastic wrap and refrigerate it until you are ready to frost the cake.

When the toothpick comes out clean, remove the cakes from the oven and set the cake pans on a cooling rack. Let them completely cool. When they are completely cool, lift them carefully by the parchment paper and rest them on cooling racks until you are ready to frost them.

When you are ready to frost them, transfer one cake to a cake stand or platter. Frost the top of the cake. Carefully stack the second cake on top of the first. Frost the top of the 2nd layer and the sides of the cake. If there is extra frosting, enjoy!

Decorate with chopped walnuts on the side of the cake. Place a small amount of chopped walnuts in your hand and gently pat your open hand along the sides of the cake – the walnuts should stick to the frosting.

Keep the cake refrigerated so the frosting stays firm. It tastes even better after it's been in the fridge.

Nutritious Carrot Cake With Creamy Lemon Orange Frosting

This carrot cake is packed full of fresh nutritious goodness and bursting with delicious flavors such as sweet carrots, ginger, orange, lemon, cinnamon, and vanilla. Of course carrot cake wouldn't be complete without a creamy lemon and orange cashew frosting! Cashews are a great alternative to cream cheese. When soaked and blended, they become a smooth and creamy texture similar to cream cheese frosting.

Ingredients

For the Cake:

1 1/2 cups oat flour (Simply blend oats into flour)

3 cups grated carrots

2 cups Medjool dates, seeds removed

1/2 cup macadamia nuts or nuts of choice

1/2 cup freshly juiced orange

1/2 zest of an orange

1 1/2 tablespoons grated ginger

1 tablespoon coconut oil

1 teaspoon cinnamon

1/2 teaspoon vanilla powder

To Make the Creamy Icing:

2 cups cashews

1 cup coconut cream or milk, refrigerated overnight

5 Medjool dates, seeds removed

1/2 medium-sized orange, juiced

1 medium-sized lemon, juiced

1 tablespoon orange zest

1 tablespoon lemon zest

1/2 teaspoon vanilla powder

1/2 teaspoon cinnamon

2 tablespoons coconut oil

Dash of maple syrup

For Garnish:

Pumpkin seeds

Grated carrot

Pistachios

Maple syrup

Preparation

Soak the cashews for 2 or more hours in water.

I like to make the frosting first so it can cool in the refrigerator. Simply blend all icing ingredients until smooth, pour into a bowl, and set in refrigerator.

Blend all cake ingredients until well combined.

Line the bottom of a springform cake tin with baking paper and transfer half of the cake mixture into the tin and smooth out with a spoon.

Take the frosting out of the refrigerator and transfer half of the mixture onto the cake, smooth out with spoon and place in freezer for about 2 hours or until the frosting has hardened.

Transfer the rest of the cake mixture onto the icing layer and smooth out with a spoon. Place back in freezer for at least an hour to harden slightly.

When you are ready to serve, take out of the freezer, gently remove the cake from tin using a butter knife to loosen around the edges and place on a cake serving plate.

Top with remaining frosting and decorate with pumpkin seeds, grated carrot, pistachios, and a drizzle of maple syrup.

Store in refrigerator or in freezer to keep for longer however take out of the freezer for at least 15 minutes before serving.

Carrot Dark Cake

Ingredients

175g light muscovado sugar

175ml sunflower oil

3 large eggs, lightly beaten

140g grated carrot (about 3 medium)

100g raisins

1 large orange, zested

175g self-raising flour

1 tsp bicarbonate of soda

1 tsp ground cinnamon

½ tsp grated nutmeg (freshly grated will give you the best flavour)

For the frosting

175g icing sugar

1½-2 tbsp orange juice

Method

STEP 1

Heat the oven to 180C/160C fan/gas 4. Oil and line the base and sides of an 18cm square cake tin with baking parchment.

STEP 2

Tip the sugar, sunflower oil and eggs into a big mixing bowl. Lightly mix with a wooden spoon. Stir in the carrots, raisins and orange zest.

STEP 3

Sift the flour, bicarbonate of soda, cinnamon and nutmeg into the bowl. Mix everything together, the mixture will be soft and almost runny.

STEP 4

Pour the mixture into the prepared tin and bake for 40-45 mins or until it feels firm and springy when you press it in the centre.

STEP 5

Cool in the tin for 5 mins, then turn it out, peel off the paper and cool on a wire rack. (You can freeze the cake at this point if you want to serve it at a later date.)

STEP 6

Beat the icing sugar and orange juice in a small bowl until smooth – you want the icing about as runny as single cream. Put the cake on a serving plate and boldly drizzle the icing back and forth in diagonal lines over the top, letting it drip down the sides.

Classic Carrot Cake

Ingredients

For the carrot cake

450ml/16fl oz vegetable oil

400g/14oz plain flour

2 tsp bicarbonate of soda

550g/1lb 4oz sugar

5 free-range eggs

½ tsp salt

2½ tsp ground cinnamon

525g/1lb 3oz carrots, grated

150g/5½oz shelled walnuts, chopped

For the icing

200g/7oz cream cheese

150g/5½oz caster sugar

100g/3½oz butter, softened

How-to-videos

Method

For the carrot cake, preheat the oven to 180C/160C Fan/Gas 4. Grease and line a 26cm/10in springform cake tin.

Mix all of the ingredients for the carrot cake, except the carrots and walnuts, together in a bowl until well combined. Stir in the carrots and walnuts.

Spoon the mixture into the cake tin and bake for 1 hour 15 minutes, or until a skewer inserted into the middle comes out clean. Remove the cake from the oven and set aside to cool for 10 minutes, then carefully remove the cake from the tin and set aside to cool completely on a cooling rack.

Meanwhile, for the icing, beat the cream cheese, caster sugar and butter together in a bowl until fluffy. Spread the icing over the top of the cake with a palette knife.

Epic Gluten Free Carrot Cake

The sponge itself happens to be dairy free, so it could also be used as a base for a dairy free gluten free carrot cake if you adjust the topping. Lactose free bakers can simply use lactose free butter and cream cheese.

Dairy free bakers might consider a coconut-based frosting, which would go beautifully with the flavours and spices in this gluten free carrot cake.

I have made this carrot cake for a couple of birthdays now, creating a triple-layer carrot cake sponge. To make this as a celebration cake, simply increase the quantities by 50% and you'll have enough batter and icing for a three layer sponge cake.

Ingredients

For the cake

200g light brown sugar

2 large eggs

180ml sunflower oil

20ml orange juice

1 tsp vanilla essence

200g gluten free self-raising flour

0.5 tsp xanthan gum

1 tsp bicarbonate of soda

0.5 tsp gluten free baking powder

1 tsp cinnamon

0.5 tsp ground ginger

0.5 tsp salt

200g grated carrot

100g chopped pecans or walnuts (I prefer pecans)

Zest of 1 orange

For the cream cheese frosting:

Zest of half a lime

450g icing sugar

70g butter

200g cream cheese

For the topping:

50g pistachios/walnuts/pecans

Zest of half a lime

Instructions

Preheat the oven to 170C (fan). Take two cake tins (approx 20cm) and lightly grease the edges with butter or oil, then line the base of each with non-stick baking paper.

In a large bowl, mix the eggs and the sifted light brown sugar until well combined.

Add the sunflower oil, orange juice and vanilla essence to the eggs and sugar - mix.

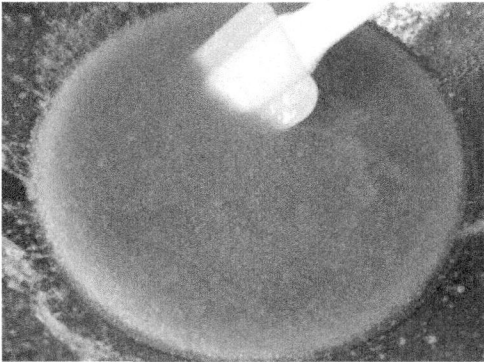

Now sift the following ingredients into the bowl: self raising flour, xanthan gum, bicarbonate, baking powder, cinnamon, ginger and salt. Use a wooden spoon or spatula to stir all together until everything is well combined and any lumps in the mixture have been smoothed out.

Stir in the grated carrot, orange zest and chopped nuts to distribute them evenly throughout the gluten free carrot cake mixture.

Divide the mixture between the two cake tins, using a spatula or spoon to gently push the cake batter to the edges of the tin.

These go into the oven on the middle shelf, to bake for 30 minutes or until your cake tester comes out clean when inserted into the centre of the cakes.

Remove from the oven and leave to cool in the tin for 5 minutes.

Then gently run a spatula around the edge of the tins before carefully tipping the carrot cakes out onto a wire rack to cool completely.

Once the gluten free carrot cakes have fully cooled, you can make the cream cheese frosting and start assembling the cake.

In a clean bowl, mix your butter with a wooden spoon or electric whisk until it is soft and smooth. You should be using slightly chilled butter if possible as this tends to yield a nice thick icing.

Add the cream cheese to the butter and mix well to combine. Then you gradually mix in the sifted icing sugar - doing this gradually will help avoid any lumps forming. I would use a wooden spoon to initially mix the icing sugar in, then if you have an electric whisk this is handy for giving everything a final blend. You should end up with a lovely smooth frosting.

Finally, add the lime zest to the frosting and stir it through until you have a nice even distribution.

Now to assemble the gluten free carrot cake. Place the first sponge on your serving plate or board and top with half of the cream cheese frosting. Use a palette knife to spread it right to the edges.

Place the second sponge on top of the first and top with the remaining cream cheese frosting. Spread to the edges with a palette knife.

Sprinkle the chopped nuts of your choosing on top of the cake, along with the remaining lime zest. I like to concentrate the nuts in the centre then sprinkle them more sparsely around the edges, for a nice effect. And there you have it - epic gluten free carrot cake that is ready for eating!

Carrot Cake Cupcakes with Cream Cheese Frosting

I've adapted my epic gluten free carrot cake recipe to cupcake form! These lovely soft cupcakes are full of nuts and tasty flavours, then topped with lusciously smooth cream cheese frosting (droooooool). I am slightly obsessed with this recipe already haha!

Loads of you love making the full cake, but downsizing to gluten free carrot cake cupcake form means that you can make a smaller quantity if you wish. The recipe here is for 12 cupcakes, simply halve it for a smaller batch and it will work just as well.

Ingredients

For the cupcakes:

200g light brown sugar

2 large eggs

180ml sunflower oil

20ml orange juice

1 tsp vanilla essence

200g gluten free self-raising flour

0.5 tsp xanthan gum

1 tsp bicarbonate of soda

0.5 tsp gluten free baking powder

1 tsp cinnamon

0.5 tsp ground ginger

0.5 tsp fine salt

200g grated carrot

100g chopped pecans (walnuts also fine)

Zest of 1 orange

For the cream cheese frosting:

Zest of half a lime

450g icing sugar

70g butter

200g cream cheese

For the topping:

50g pistachios/walnuts/pecans

Zest of half a lime

Instructions

Preheat the oven to 170C (fan). Take a 12-hole muffin tin and line with muffin cases.

In a large bowl, mix the eggs and the sifted light brown sugar until well combined.

Add the sunflower oil, orange juice and vanilla essence to the eggs and sugar - mix.

Now sift the following ingredients into the bowl: self raising flour, xanthan gum, bicarbonate, baking powder, cinnamon, ginger and salt. Use a wooden spoon or spatula to stir all together until everything is well combined and any lumps in the mixture have been smoothed out.

Stir in the grated carrot (coarse or finely grated both okay), orange zest and chopped nuts to distribute them evenly throughout the gluten free carrot cake mixture.

Divide the mixture between the muffin cases (each should be approx two thirds full), using a spoon to gently level the batter. Pop the tray on the middle shelf of your oven and bake for 25 minutes or until your cake tester comes out clean when inserted into the centre of your tester cupcake.

Remove from the oven and transfer the cupcakes to a wire rack to cool completely. Once they have cooled, you can make the cream cheese frosting, mmm!

In a clean bowl, mix your butter with a wooden spoon or electric whisk until it has been whipped smooth.

Add the cream cheese to the butter and mix well to combine. Then you gradually mix in the sifted icing sugar - doing this gradually will help avoid any lumps forming. I would use a wooden spoon to initially mix the icing sugar in, then if you have an electric whisk this is handy for giving everything a final blitz. You should end up with a lovely smooth, thick frosting.

Finally, add the lime zest to the frosting and stir it through until you have a nice even distribution.

Now to ice your cupcakes! Add a heaped tsp of frosting to each cupcake, then use a small palette knife to spread it across the surface and create a pretty swirl. Sprinkle some chopped nuts on top of each cupcake, along with the remaining lime zest and then eat :D.

Easy Carrot Cake

Ingredients:

3 eggs

300g sugar

1/2 tsp salt

128 g oil

190g all-purpose flour

1/2 tsp baking powder

3/4 tsp baking soda

1 pinch cinnamon powder

343g shredded carrots

30g golden raisins

60g walnuts

Step-by-step:

Heat oven to 170C

Mix the oil, eggs, sugar into a large mixing bowl. Quickly mix with an electric whisk until smooth.

Once done, prepare your flour mixture. Mix salt, baking powder, baking soda and cinnamon powder.

Gradually add the flour mixture to the mixer bowl. Make sure that it is mixed until the batter comes together.

Add shredded carrots, raisins and walnuts to the mixer bowl.

Once it is all mixed, scrape the batter into your preferred tin.

Bake the Carrot Cake in the oven for 25 mins until golden.

For bigger cakes, cool in the tin for a day before decorating.

Pro-tip: Use a skewer to poke into the cake to check if its ready. Once it comes out clean and dry, your cake is ready!

Time to make your delicious Carrot Cake look good too. Turn it into a divine dessert treat with some Cream Cheese Frosting and top it with colourful edible art.

Ingredient:

250g cream cheese

83g butter

83g icing sugar

1 lemon zest

Step-by-step

Beat cream cheese in a mixing bowl with an electric whisk until smooth. Make sure to remove all lumps.

Add lemon zest, butter and icing sugar. Make sure everything's mixed well.

To make it colourful, add edible food dyes to your frosting and decorate it!

Super Moist Carrot Cake

INGREDIENTS:

For Cake:

2 cups sifted flour

2 teaspoons baking powder

1½ teaspoons baking soda

1½ teaspoons salt

2 teaspoons ground cinnamon

1 teaspoon ground ginger

½ teaspoon freshly grated nutmeg

1½ cups sugar

1½ cups canola oil

4 eggs

2 cups finely grated carrot

1 can (250 grams) of crushed pineapple, drained

For Cream Cheese Frosting:

½ cup butter

1 cup cream cheese

2 teaspoons vanilla extract

28 grams icing sugar, sifted

INSTRUCTIONS:

1. Preheat your oven to 180°C and grease three 9-inch round cake pans.

2. Sift together the flour, baking powder, baking soda, salt, ginger, nutmeg and cinnamon. Then add the sugar, canola oil, and eggs; mix well

3. Next add the carrot and pineapple. Blend thoroughly.

4. Distribute the batter evenly among the three pans.

5. Bake the cakes for 35-40 minutes. Be careful not to over-bake them.

6. Remove the pans from the oven and cool for 15-20 minutes before turning out onto wire racks to cool completely.

7. When your cakes have cooled, make your cream cheese frosting by mixing all the ingredients together in a bowl using an electric mixer while gradually adding the icing sugar.

8. Finally frost the cake and spread a thin layer between each layer of cake.

Serve and enjoy! Happy baking!

Carrot cake with cream-cheese frosting

INGREDIENTS

2 cups (300g) self-raising flour

1 1/2 cups (225g) plain flour

1 teaspoon bicarbonate of soda

2 1/2 teaspoons ground cinnamon

2 1/2 teaspoons ground nutmeg

2 cups (440g) caster sugar

3 1/2 cups coarsely grated carrot

100g walnuts, roughly chopped

1 1/4 cups (310ml) vegetable oil

5 eggs, lightly beaten

300g sour cream

2 teaspoons vanilla extract

CREAM CHEESE FROSTING

500g cream cheese, softened

1 teaspoon vanilla extract

3 1/3 cups (500g) icing sugar

CANDIED CARROT

1 large carrot, shredded lengthways using a zester, plus 1 small carrot

1 cup (220g) caster sugar

1 green jelly snake, cut into thin strips

METHOD

1. Preheat oven to 180°C. Grease and line a 25cm round cake pan with baking paper.

2. Sift flours, soda and spices into a large bowl. Add caster sugar, grated carrot and walnuts and stir to combine.

3. In a separate bowl, whisk oil, eggs, sour cream and vanilla until smooth.

4. Add to dry ingredients and stir until just combined. Pour into pan, smoothing top with a spatula. Bake in the oven for 2 hours or until a

skewer inserted into the centre comes out clean. Stand for 20 minutes, then turn out onto a rack to cool.

5. For frosting, beat cream cheese using electric beaters until smooth. Add vanilla and beat well. Gradually add icing sugar, beating until smooth and creamy.

6. Split cooled cake into 2 layers. Spread bottom layer with half the frosting. Add top, then spread with remaining frosting.

7. For candied carrot, cut a 4cm piece from the end of the small carrot and use a vegetable peeler to make a small carrot shape. Place sugar and 1 cup (250ml) water in a pan over low heat, stirring to dissolve sugar. Add the mini carrot and simmer for 1-2 minutes until just tender. Remove and set aside. Add the shredded carrot to the pan and cook for 3-4 minutes until candied and transparent. Remove and set aside. Turn heat to medium and allow liquid to bubble for 1-2 minutes until reduced and syrupy, then remove from heat. Add mini carrot and shreds and allow to cool. To decorate, drain carrot and shreds on paper towel. Spread shreds around edge of frosted cake. Place mini carrot in centre, then arrange snake strips as leaves.

Printed in Great Britain
by Amazon

27135759R00040